Published simultaneously in 1995 by Exley Publications in Great Britain, and Exley Giftbooks in the USA.

12 11 10 9 8 7 6 5 4 3 2 1

Copyright © Exley Publications 1995

ISBN 1-85015-526-7

Edited and pictures selected by Dalton Exley.
Designed by Pinpoint Design Company.
Pictures researched by P. A. Goldberg and J. M. Clift, Image Select, London.
Typesetting by Delta, Watford.
Printed by Kossuth Printing House Co. in Hungary.

Exley Publications Ltd, 16 Chalk Hill, Watford, Herts WD1 4BN, United Kingdom.
Exley Giftbooks, 232 Madison Avenue, Suite 1206, NY 10016, USA.

Acknowledgements: The publishers are grateful for permission to reproduce copyright material, Whilst every effort has been made to trace copyright holders, Exley Publications would be happy to hear from any copyright holder not here acknowledged.
Wendell Berry: extract from "Collected Poems" © 1980 Wendell Berry; Thornkild Bjornvig: extract from "The Owl" cited in "News Of The Universe" © 1980 Robert Bly, Sierra Club Books; Rachel Carson: extract from "Silent Spring" © Rachel L. Carson 1962 published by Hamish Hamilton Ltd. Reprinted by permission of Laurence Pollinger Ltd.; Rick Fields: extract from "Chop Wood, Carry Water" by Rick Fields, Peggy Taylor, Rex Weyler and Rick Ingrasci, published by Jeremy P. Tarcher Inc., © 1984 Rick Fields, Rex Weyler, Rick Ingrasci and Peggy Taylor; Mahatma Gandhi: extracts from "The Words Of Gandhi", selected by Sir Richard Attenborough, published by Newmarket Press, USA © 1982; Yuri Glazkov: extract from "The Home Planet" published by Macdonald/Queen Anne Press © Kevin W. Kelley 1988. Reprinted by permission of Headline Book Publishing plc; Paul Hyland: extract from "The Stubborn Forest" published by Bloodaxe Books (UK), 1984 © Paul Hyland 1984; Mary Oliver: extract from "Dream Work" © Atlantic Monthly Press, USA; Jonathon Porritt: extract from "Save The Earth" published by Dorling Kindersley © 1991 Dorling Kindersley and Jonathon Porritt; Barbara Ward and Rene Dubos: extracts from "Only One Earth" published by André Deutsch, 1972 © The Report On The Human Environment Inc. 1972.
Picture Credits: Exley Publications is very grateful to the following individuals and organizations for permission to reproduce their pictures: Archiv fur Kunst (AKG), Art Resource (AR), Bridgeman Art Library (BAL), Edimedia (EDM), Fine Art Photographic Library (FAP), Giraudon (GIR), Zefa Picture Library (ZPL). Cover: Leistikow (AKG); title page; Camille Pissarro, Mannheim Art Gallery (BAL); page 6: © 1995 Adrian Stokes, "Autumn in the Mountains" (BAL); page 8: John Atkinson Grimshaw, Christopher Wood Gallery (BAL); page 10: H. E. Cross (EDM); page 13: Leistikow (AKG); page 14/15: Jean Francois Millet (AKG); page 16: Gustav Klimt (AKG); page 18/19: Fernand Khnopff, Whitford & Hughes, London (BAL); page 20/21: Valentin Serow (AKG); page 23: Lucien Frank, by courtesy Galerie Berko (FAP); page 25: Pierre Auguste Renoir, Christie's, London (BAL); page 26: Vincent van Gogh (AKG); page 29: Henri Delacroix (ZPL); page 30/31: Paul Gauguin (EDM); page 32: Vincent van Gogh, Metropolitan Museum of Art, N.Y. (EDM); page 34: Gustave Courbet (AKG); page 36: John Byam Liston (BAL); page 39: Vanessa Bell, Bonhams, London (BAL); page 41: Camille Pissarro, Mannheim Art Gallery (BAL); page 42/43: Timothy Easton, Private Collection (BAL); page 44/45: Curt Hermann (AKG); page 46: Paul Gauguin (GIR/AR); page 49: © 1995 Lamorna-Birch, Galerie George, London (BAL); page 50/51: John Edward Newton (AKG); page 52/53 : Camille Pissarro, Musée d'Orsay (GIR/BAL); 54/55: Vincent van Gogh (EDM); page 56/57: Archip Kuindski (AKG); page 58: Vincent van Gogh (AR); page 60/61: Vincent van Gogh (AKG).

THE BEST OF
NATURE
QUOTATIONS

EDITED BY
DALTON EXLEY

NEW YORK • WATFORD, UK

Peaceful, the gentle deer untroubled graze:
All that they need,
their forest-home supplies.
No greed for wealth nor envy
clouds their days.
But these are only beasts, and we are wise.

BHARTRIHARI, *from "Poems from the Sanskrit"*

"...is this not a precious home for all of us earthlings? Is it not worth our love? Does it not deserve all the inventiveness and courage and generosity of which we are capable to preserve it from degradation and destruction and, by doing so, to secure our own survival?"

BARBARA WARD (1914 - 1981) and RENÉ DUBOS (1901 - 1982)

"...this curious world which we inhabit is more wonderful than it is convenient; more beautiful than it is useful; it is more to be admired and enjoyed than used."

HENRY DAVID THOREAU (1817 – 1862)

...nature is never spent;
There lives the dearest freshness deep down things...

GERARD MANLEY HOPKINS (1844 – 1889), *from "God's Grandeur"*

"...nature itself means nothing, says nothing except to the perceiving mind.... Beauty is where it is perceived...you surely will see...if you are prepared to see it – if you look for it..."

HENRY DAVID THOREAU (1817 - 1862)

"It is only in exceptional minds that we realize how wonderful are the commonest experiences of life. It seems to me sometimes that these experiences have an 'inner' side, as well as the outer side we normally perceive. At such moments one suddenly sees everything with new eyes; one feels on the brink of some great revelation. It is as if we caught a glimpse of some incredibly beautiful world that lies silently about us all the time."

J. W. N. SULLIVAN

"...we're paying too high a price for what we call 'progress'. It is not just the Earth that has paid the price of our obsessive pursuit of industrial progress, but that fragile part of us that responds to a higher reality than material wealth."

JONATHON PORRITT

"The earth's distances invite the eye. And
as the eye reaches, so must the mind
stretch to meet these new horizons. I
challenge anyone to stand with autumn on
a hilltop and fail to see a new expanse not
only around him, but in him, too."

HAL BORLAND

There is a pleasure in the pathless woods,
   There is a rapture on the lonely shore,
   There is society, where none intrudes,
   By the deep Sea, and music in its roar:
O love not Man the less, but Nature more,
From these our interviews, in which I steal
   For all I may be, or have been before,
   To mingle with the Universe, and feel
      What I can ne'er express,
      yet can not all conceal.

LORD BYRON (1788 - 1824),
excerpt from "The Ocean", from "Childe Harold's Pilgrimage"

No plot so narrow, be but Nature there,
No waste so vacant, but may well employ
Each faculty of sense, and keep the heart
   Awake to Love and Beauty!

SAMUEL TAYLOR COLERIDGE (1772 - 1834)

"Those who contemplate the beauty of the
Earth find reserves of strength that will
endure as long as life lasts.
There is symbolic as well as actual
beauty in the migration of birds,
the ebb and flow of tides, the folded
bud ready for spring.
There is something infinitely healing in the
repeated refrains of nature – the
assurance that dawn comes after the night
and spring after the winter."

RACHEL CARSON (1907 - 1964), *from "Silent Spring"*

PROUD SONGSTERS

These are brand-new birds of
twelve-months' growing,
Which a year ago, or less than twain,
No finches were, nor nightingales,
Nor thrushes,
But only particles of grain,
And earth and air, and rain.

THOMAS HARDY (1840 - 1928)

And where is voice
So young, so beautiful, and sweet
As nature's choice,
Where spring and lovers meet?
JOHN CLARE (1793 - 1864)

·"A vision without a task is but a
dream, a task without a vision is
drudgery, a vision and a task is the
hope of the world."

FROM A CHURCH IN SUSSEX, ENGLAND, c.1730

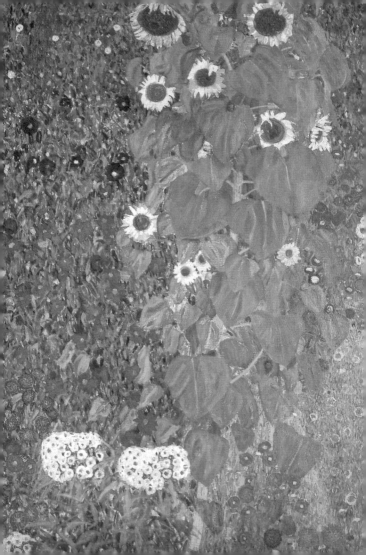

...Powerful grace that lies
In herbs, plants, stones, and their qualities:
For naught so vile that on the
earth doth live
But to the earth some special
food doth give.
WILLIAM SHAKESPEARE (1564 - 1616)

An owl sat once with his sharp hearing,
his watchfulness,
his bill, half-grown, majestic on my finger;
then I felt his huge and yellow stare
plant something foreign in me,
a deep quiet,
a mad freedom; my heart laughed
when the bird raised his soft wings.
THORKILD BJORNVIG, *from "The Owl"*

HYMN TO EARTH, MOTHER OF ALL

Gaia, mother of all, hard, splendid as rock,
Eldest of all beings;
I sing the greatness of Earth!
Mother of gods, bride of the
starry sky, farewell!
ANONYMOUS, GREEK (6th century B.C.)

Over all the hilltops
Silence,
Among the treetops
You feel hardly
A breath moving.
The birds fall silent in the woods.
Simply wait! Soon
You too will be silent.

JOHANN WOLFGANG VON GOETHE (1749 – 1832)

The great sea
Has sent me adrift
It moves me
As the weed in a great river
Earth and the great weather
Move me
Have carried me away
And move my inward parts with joy.

UVAVNUK, *Eskimo woman shaman*

Quietening the mind,
Deep in the forest
Water drips down.
HOSHA

"We love quiet; we suffer the mouse to play; when the woods are rustled by the wind, we fear not."

INDIAN CHIEF TO THE GOVERNOR OF PENNSYLVANIA, 1796

And this our life,
exempt from public haunt,
Finds tongues in trees, books in the
running brooks,
Sermons in stones, and good in everything.
I would not change it.

WILLIAM SHAKESPEARE (1564 - 1616), *from "As You Like It"*

Some nights, stay up till dawn...
Be a full bucket pulled up the dark way
of a well, then lifted out into light.

Something opens our wings. Something
makes boredom and hurt disappear.
Something fills the cup in front of us.
We taste only sacredness.

JALAL AD-DIN AR-RUMI, PERSIAN (c.1207 - 1273)

Grant me the ability to be alone,
May it be my custom to go outdoors each day
among the trees and grasses,
among all growing things
and there may I be alone,
and enter into prayer
to talk with the one
that I belong to.

RABBI NACHMAN OF BRATZLAV

"I am particularly fond of the little groves of oak trees. I love to look at them, because they endure the wintry storm and the summer's heat, and – not unlike ourselves – seem to flourish by them."

TATANKA YOTANKA or SITTING BULL (1834 - 1890)

"...a love [for his native soil] wholly mystical. He used to say [that] healthy feet can hear the very heart of Holy Earth.... Up always before dawn, he liked to bathe his bare feet, walking about in the morning dew."

a biographer writing about Sitting Bull

"Behold my brothers, the spring has come; the earth has received the embraces of the sun and we shall soon see the results of that love! Every seed is awakened and so has all animal life. It is through this mysterious power that we too have our being and we therefore yield to our neighbors, even our animal neighbors, the same right as ourselves, to inhabit this land."

TATANKA YOTANKE or SITTING BULL (1834 - 1890)

A child said, What is the grass?

And now it seems to me the beautiful
uncut hair of graves...
The smallest sprout shows
there is really no death,
And if ever there was it led forward life,
and does not wait at the end to arrest it...

This is the grass that grows wherever the
land is and the water is,
This is the common air that bathes
the globe.

I believe a leaf of grass is no less than the
journey-work of the stars...
And a mouse a miracle enough to stagger
sextillions of infidels.

WALT WHITMAN (1819 - 1891), *from "Song Of Myself"*

I swear the earth shall surely be complete
to him or her who shall be complete,
The earth remains jagged and broken only
to him or her who remains jagged and
broken.

WALT WHITMAN (1819-1891)

"If the Earth were only a few feet in diameter, floating a few feet above a field somewhere, people would come from everywhere to marvel at it.... The people would marvel at all the creatures walking around the surface of the ball and at the creatures in the water. The people would declare it as sacred because it was the only one, and they would protect it so that it would not be hurt. The ball would be the greatest wonder known, and people would come to pray to it, to be healed, to gain knowledge, to know beauty and to wonder how it could be."

JOE MILLER

Hast never come to thee an hour,
A sudden gleam divine, precipitating,
bursting all these bubbles,
fashions, wealth?
These eager business aims – books,
politics, art, amours,
To utter nothingness?

WALT WHITMAN (1819 - 1891)

Go out, go out I beg of you
And taste the beauty of the wild.
Behold the miracle of the earth
With all the wonder of a child.
EDNA JAQUES

"Change, individuation, metamorphosis, transmigration of form – all these point to growth itself, not the grown thing, as the great underlying reality in nature."

HENRY DAVID THOREAU (1817 - 1862)

You do not have to be good.
You do not have to walk on your knees
for a hundred miles through the desert,
repenting.
You only have to let the soft animal of your
body love what it loves.
Tell me about despair, yours, and I will tell
you mine.
Meanwhile the world goes on.
Meanwhile the sun and the clear pebbles of
the rain
are moving across the landscapes,
over the prairies and the deep trees,
the mountains and the rivers.
Meanwhile the wild geese, high up in the
clean blue air,
are heading home again.
Whoever you are, no matter how lonely,
the world offers itself to your imagination,
calls to you like the wild geese, harsh and
exciting –
over and over announcing your place
in the family of things.

MARY OLIVER

"Hills are always more beautiful than stone buildings, you know. Living in a city is an artificial existence. Lots of people hardly ever feel real soil under their feet, see plants grow except in flower pots, or get far enough beyond the street light to catch the enchantment of a night sky studded with stars."

TATANGA MANI or WALKING BUFFALO, *a Stoney Indian*

"We who prayed and wept
for liberty from kings
and the yoke of liberty
accept the tyranny of things
we do not need.
In plenitude too free,
we have become adept
beneath the yoke of greed."

WENDELL BERRY, b.1934

Reporter: "Mr. Gandhi, what do you think of modern civilisation?"
Gandhi: "That would be a good idea!"

"Wildness made man but man cannot make wildness. He can only spare it."

DAVID BROWER

What would the world be, once bereft
Of wet and wildness? Let them be left
O let them be left, wildness and wet;
Long live the weeds and the wilderness yet.
GERARD MANLEY HOPKINS (1844 - 1889)

Nothing is so beautiful as Spring –
When weeds, in wheels, shoot long and
lovely and lush:
What is all this juice and all this joy?
GERARD MANLEY HOPKINS (1844 - 1889)

"We sleep, but the loom of life never stops
and the pattern which was weaving when
the sun went down is weaving when it
comes up to-morrow."
HENRY WARD BEECHER (1813 - 1887)

O if we but knew what we do
When we delve or hew –
Hack and rack the growing green!
Where we, even where we mean
To mend her, we end her,
When we hew or delve:
After-comers cannot guess the beauty been.
GERARD MANLEY HOPKINS (1844 - 1889),
from "Binsey Poplars" (Felled 1879)

"But indeed, it is not so much for its beauty
– that the forest makes a claim upon men's
hearts, as for that subtle something,
that quality of the air, that emanates from
the old trees, that so wonderfully changes
and renews a weary spirit."

ROBERT LOUIS STEVENSON (1850 - 1894)

SELF-MOCKERY AT THE PLANTING OF TREES

At seventy? still planting trees?
Don't laugh:
We all die, sooner or later.
But who knows when?

YUAN MEI, CHINESE (1716 - 1798)

"Trees are poems that the earth writes
upon the sky. We fell them down and
turn them into paper that we may
record our emptiness."

KAHLIL GIBRAN (1883 - 1931), *from "Sand and Foam"*

I think that I shall never see
A poem as lovely as a tree,
Poems are made by fools like me
But only God can make a tree.

ALFRED (JOYCE) KILMER

To Make A Tree

Take wood, seasoned or green,
rough-hewn or planed.
Take first one four-square beam
twice a man's height,
then graft a second, half that,
on to it
cross-wise and near the top,
cunningly joined.
Dig socket. Plant upright.
Hope it will root,
hope sap will rise. If not,
keep tools at hand
and, when the time is ripe,
nail up the fruit.

PAUL HYLAND

"Nature doth thus kindly heal every
wound. By the meditation of a thousand
little mosses and fungi, the most unsightly
objects become radiant of beauty."

RUSSELL L.SCHWEICHKART

"The poetry of the earth is never dead."

JOHN KEATS (1795 - 1821)

"No matter how deeply we look into the
fabric of material being – the biological
level, the chemical level, subatomic level –
we see that life forms are interdependent,
co-conditioning and co-evolving. Every
human effort, civilisation, thought, and
spiritual insight, requires and is supported
by the whole of organic life."

RICK FIELDS

"In those vernal seasons of the year,
when the air is calm and pleasant, it
were an injury and sullenness against
Nature not to go out, and see her riches,
and partake in her rejoicing with
heaven and earth."

JOHN MILTON (1608 - 1674)

I'm filled with joy
when the day dawns quietly
over the roof of the sky.

from an Eskimo Song

"Though we travel the world over to find the beautiful, we must carry it with us or we find it not."

ANONYMOUS

"We all understand that the life systems of this planet are interrelated, that our human future depends on the well-being of the rain forest and the salt marsh. We know that human activity in the production of goods and services can damage and destroy the environment on which we and our children depend. We know all these intellectually.... And we fear together the misuse of the power we have now at our collective fingertips through our amazing technology."

BARBARA WARD (1914 - 1981)

"Evolution has shown us that nothing ever stays the same: continents drift across the oceans, jungles turn into deserts, and dinosaurs make way for silky anteaters. And where the wind and the sun once dictated the course of evolution, the near future of this planet resides in the mind and action of man. The balancing of and the struggle between greed, compassion, fear, and intelligence will now determine the destiny of all life on Earth."

CHARLES LYNN BRAGG

"Humans ... have never been helpless. They have only been deflected or deceived or dispirited. This is not to say their history has not been pockmarked by failure. But failure is not the ultimate fact of life; it is an aspect of life in which transient or poor judgments play larger roles than they should."

NORMAN COUSINS

"We must establish a concept of security that can deal with the threats from poverty and environmental degradation at the same level of attention and priority as has been given to the danger from war."

GRO HARLEM BRUNDTLAND

"A good idea that is not shared with others will gradually fade away and bear no fruit, but when it is shared it lives forever because it is passed on from one person to another and grows as it goes."

LOWELL FILLMORE

"Almost anything you do will seem insignificant, but it is very important that you do it."

MAHATMA GANDHI (1869 - 1948)

TO LIANG QICHAO

Land of wealth, land of beauty,
Sinking fast – and who can save her?
My tears! My worry!
Oh, but where has my country come to?
This heart, this strength,
Will never give in, will never give up!

HUANG ZUNXIAN, CHINESE (1848 - 1905)

I am only one,
But still I am one.
I cannot do everything,
But still I can do something;
And because I cannot do everything
I will not refuse to do the something
that I can do.

EDWARD E. HALE (1822 - 1909)

"In my humble opinion, non-cooperation
with evil is as much a duty as is
cooperation with good."

MAHATMA GANDHI (1869 - 1948)

Holy Mother Earth, the trees and all
nature are witnesses of your
thoughts and deeds.

A WINNEBAGO WISE SAYING

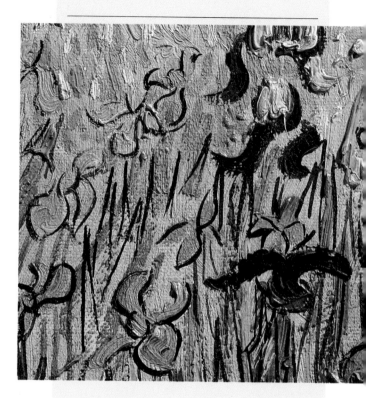

"We must shed the quaint superstition that ours is a race in some special way entitled to exploit this planet ad infinitum for its own selfish purpose...."

KARAN SINGH

"I want to realize brotherhood or identity
not merely with the beings called human,
but I want to realize identity with all life,
even with such beings as crawl on earth."

MAHATMA GANDHI (1869 - 1948)

"Photographed from the moon, [the earth]
seems to be a kind of organism. It is plainly
in the process of developing, like an
enormous embryo. It is, for all its
stupendous size and the numberless units
of its life forms, coherent.
Every tissue is linked for its viability
to every other tissue."

LEWIS THOMAS, *from "The Medusa and the Snail"*

"Nature has been limitlessly kind to us, having helped humankind appear, stand up, and grow stronger. She has generously given us everything she has amassed over the billions of years of inanimate development. We have grown strong and powerful, yet how have we answered this goodness?"

YURI GLAZKOV

"...some furrows in a ploughed field – a bit of sand, sea and sky – are serious subjects, so difficult, but at the same time so beautiful, that it is indeed worth while to devote one's life to expressing the poetry hidden in them."

VINCENT VAN GOGH (1853 - 1890), *from Letters Volume 1*

"The tree which moves some to tears of joy is in the Eyes of others only a Green thing that stands in the way. Some see Nature all Ridicule and Deformity ... & Some Scarce see Nature at all. But to the Eyes of the Man of Imagination, Nature is Imagination itself."

WILLIAM BLAKE (1757 - 1827)

"The earth is not ... a mere fragment of dead history, strata upon strata, like the leaves of a book, an object for a museum and an antiquarian, but living poetry like the leaves of a tree, – not a fossil earth, but a living specimen."

HENRY DAVID THOREAU (1817 - 1862)

It is only a little planet
But how beautiful it is.
ROBINSON JEFFERS

"If one really loves nature, one can find beauty everywhere."
VINCENT VAN GOGH (1853 - 1890)